You Are the Consumer

Chart Your Path and Lead the Way in the New Music Business

Kayode Badmus-Wellington

Cunningham
Labs

To Mama, who beat cancer three times over the past decade—overcoming blood cancer (MDS) last year through a stem cell transplant, which I was honored to be the donor for. You sparked the idea for this book, reminding me always that my perspective is valuuble and to follow my passions. Your strength, intelligence, resilience, and joy for life are my greatest inspirations. I love you.

To my fiancée, Sheeva, for believing in me, grounding me, and loving me through every single twist and turn. You've shown me a new way of living. Your love is my driving force, and I couldn't imagine who or where I'd be without you.

To Daddy and Sarah—thank you for always encouraging me, having my back, and accepting me for who I am. Your love of music centers me, and it's always been one of my biggest motivations, reminding me of why I started this journey two decades ago and why I continue to push forward every day.

To everyone who's stood by me, cheered me on, and valued my perspective—thank you.

Table of Contents

Introduction

When I first sought out to write an essay about the music business, I really didn't have a clue about what I wanted to discuss. I just knew it had been a dream of mine to write and publish an essay about the business in an industry trade. Honestly, I thought it was cool—the idea of shaping and contributing to the storyline of the business I'd been enamored with since I was a little kid. That essay ended up being titled *The Essence of A&R: We Are the Consumer* and was published by *Billboard*.

As I began writing, one thing led to another (and another), and my curiosity took over. It wasn't until I got to the last paragraph that I stumbled upon the concept of "we are the consumer." Suddenly, it clicked. I found myself through that essay, but I didn't realize that was why I had to write it in the first place. It was a turning point, ultimately the universe's way of shifting me into a higher perspective about music, its influence, and my place in it. How about that? This was an idea initially born out of my frustration with how the business was operating that turned into the exact feeling I never knew I'd been chasing all along. I had been more focused on controlling the circumstances rather than influencing them. For years, the industry that I coveted appeared to have shifted away from its core of creative development and grandeur in favor of chasing trends and data supremacy.

At that point, I'd spent the majority of my life nurturing my obsession for music and ambition to participate in its evolution. When I was seventeen I even unironically got a tattoo that read "Ambition" in the font of Wale's second studio album cover merely two weeks upon my return from GRAMMY Camp. As I finally gathered the skill set, experience, and network to really make an impact, I was thrust right back to the drawing board and into a journey of self-realization. It was a testing realization, marked by several disappointments and trying moments, but there was also an underlying sense of excitement that felt uncomfortably obvious. I'd attached so much of life's weight to my passion to the point where my passion had simply given in to the pressure. I had fallen out of love with music, although as I started to accept this painful truth, the path forward became clearer. I drowned out the noise and decided to return to the basics.

Music has been synonymous with my life for as long as I can remember. I grew up in a quiet Los Angeles suburb to a Black American mother and Nigerian-immigrant father.

My mom worked in education, my dad in sales, and neither of them played instruments nor were they inherently
"musical" in the traditional sense. Yet my earliest memories
were centered around music, and the joy it brought to my
family was well ingrained. No one (and I mean no one) has
rhythm as effortless as my mom. Neither does anyone have
as broad of musical taste as my dad. My little sister is the
singer in the family. I was an introverted, neurodivergent
kid who struggled with focus, but music was always something that lit up my excitement and consumed my attention
like nothing else. It was just always on—from the car to TV,
106 & Park, MTV—and I quickly noticed how it changed
with different moods and environments. It was the first
thing I was compelled to understand and had become my
gateway to participate in the world.

By the time I was nine and picked up DJing, it was
simply the only next step to take. I'd gone from the average
consumer listening to music to ripping it, creating playlists,
burning CDs, and back to listening. Before I knew it, I was
spinning the 1s and 2s, having DJed hundreds of events and
was producing songs for local artists out of my bedroom.
It felt incredibly rewarding, and I was having a lot of fun.
When I graduated high school, you couldn't tell me I wasn't
going to be the next Pharrell. I had zero plans for college,
which had been the case since freshman year of high school.
"Why would I go into debt over a degree I know I'll never
need?" was the thinking.

Given my mom's career in education, I'm sure you can
understand she wasn't thrilled, but to her credit, she always
granted me the trust and confidence to make my own deci-

sions. After a series of unpaid recording studio internships, I determined I needed to get closer to the decision-makers to ultimately solidify my place in the business. A major record label internship became my new target, but due to a previous lawsuit involving unpaid internships, I couldn't qualify unless I was able to receive college credit. Imagine my mom's excitement when I filled her in on my new higher education plans…

Upon enrolling in the Entertainment Business bachelor's program at the Los Angeles Film School, I began doom-scrolling job sites, blindly applying to every single A&R internship I could find. About halfway through my three-year college stint, while in class, I received a call from an unlisted Beverly Hills number. At this point, I wouldn't have necessarily referred to myself as a spiritual person, but what I did know was something from within had nudged me to step outside to answer it. When I answered I was greeted by the friendly voice of someone at Sony Music asking if I'd like to interview for an internship at Epic Records. I'd been waiting for what felt like my entire life for an opportunity like this, so it wasn't something I was going to squander. As I walked into Sony's glass I.M. Pei building in Beverly Hills (the famed former CAA headquarters) at 9830 Wilshire, I had a pit in my stomach. This was it, my chance to prove myself. That A&R internship at Epic ended up changing my life.

Eleven months into my internship, I was hired on as an A&R assistant by one of my mentors, Chris Anokute. Chris is a Nigerian American A&R executive and artist development specialist whose original stamp on the business was placing "Pon de Replay" with Rihanna and A&Ring Katy Perry's *Teenage Dream* (one of the most successful albums of all time). I could dedicate an entire book to what he's done for me, but to keep it brief, he was the first person to validate my confidence and place in this industry. "If he believes in me, I must be doing something right." We went on to deliver projects for Fifth Harmony, Zara Larsson, Jennifer Hudson, French Montana (alongside another A&R, Zoe Young), and more.

The caveat of my experiences at Epic was that I had simultaneously stopped producing and creating music. What happened? At the time, I was subconsciously more driven by the idea of finding success rather than creating it. I was creatively drained. My first DJ gig was a sweet sixteen at a community clubhouse when I was ten. Music had always been my passion, but it always commingled with my professional aspirations. I'd spent much of my life aiming for success—it was something that always presented as a moving target, and here I was in a dream role, getting my first real shot. "This is something I need to give my all to, and producing music isn't going to help me here." Little did I know, I'd made the biggest mistake of my life, effectively deciding to diminish my creativity and discredit my perspective.

After Epic, I received an opportunity to become a publishing A&R director for Pulse Music Group. Pulse is a boutique indie publishing and record company that has always held a strong reputation of being creative-led. It was the ideal place to shape my chops as an A&R executive, as their ethos highlighted a new way of expressing my creativity. Through this experience, I also began to view creatives with great reverence. This had its pros and cons—on the one hand, I developed a deeper empathy for creatives, but on the other, it pushed me further away from my own identification as one.

I continued to advance in my career, finding some success as an A&R executive for various publishing and record companies. I also worked in artist management for a few years, searching for something I wasn't keenly aware was missing. I'd worked with or signed many incredible artists, songwriters, and producers across genres. I'd helped facilitate hit records. I'd done business with or knew many different executives I would've dreamed of meeting just a few short years before. I experienced the ins and outs of record companies, music publishers, and artist management.

So, what was the issue? I'd lost sight of my own unique potential, which had created the circumstances for what I now understand as depression. For a while, it felt like I was navigating on autopilot. I was comparing my decisions to those of my peers and putting my taste below that of the consumer. I was being convinced that the new dynamics of success in the music business had shifted, granting consumers the ultimate authority over which artists companies and executives would focus on. It felt like it was leading to the death of the creative executive, evidenced by a lack of job opportunities. "I would be much further as an executive if I just fully committed to research." "Artists can create and launch hits from their bedroom. No one cares about A&R or development anymore; it's all about data-fueled signings and quick wins." "Is this just the new reality?" My fate and confidence were coiled, rooted in external conditions rather than something from within. I allowed the destination to define my journey, blindfolded and sitting in the passenger seat of the vehicle.

Amidst the uncertainty and cries of anguish, something persisted. It was best characterized as a quiet knowing, an ability to look beyond the blindfold akin to Bran Stark in *Game of Thrones*. "Could there be a greater purpose behind all of this?" The industry's landscape was changing, and so was my understanding of what it meant to thrive in the new environment. "If consumers are to be the ultimate authority in the music business, isn't this the shift I've been preparing for my entire life?" When *Billboard* published my essay, I had worn many hats along my musical journey, starting from my childhood: consumer, DJ, producer, recording engineer, mixer, artist, studio intern, student, record label intern, A&R assistant, music publisher, A&R executive, and artist manager, culminating with my newest denotation as a writer. Maybe this was the point all along.

"What's the difference between myself and the consumer?" My journey had come full circle, leading me to a fundamental truth: you are the consumer, and you are in control of the reality you want to create. The distance between producers and consumers has never been shorter, and we'd entered one of the greatest eras of potential the music business has seen. Understanding these truths was transformative. My disappointment with the business ultimately became an essential part of my journey, prompting me to yearn for more and to reset my focus. It wasn't just about the roles I'd played or the titles I'd held. It was about recognizing the power of my unique perspective as a consumer and how it shaped my approach to the music business.

It brought me back to that introverted kid who found meaning in the world through music. The kid who would bask in quiet excitement while watching a crowd react to the subtleties of my mix choices. The kid with a D in English class freshman year at Valencia High School lost in a daydream, counting down the hours until I could rush home to stay up all night fine-tuning an idea I'd been working on. The kid starting as a center on the varsity basketball team, being scolded by his coach for skipping a summer tournament game to DJ a wedding. It reinvigorated my passion and provided a clearer path forward, reminding me that my individualized perspective and authenticity were my greatest assets. It was never about chasing trends, nor was it about achieving someone else's version of success; it was about creating meaningful experiences that resonate on a deeper level.

As I began to implement this concept in my work as an A&R executive at Def Jam, my experiences started to validate this new perspective. I realized that if I was feeling this way, others must be too. Recognizing that I am the consumer, the ultimate tastemaker, gave me confidence. "My unique perspective, what lights me up, will probably light up others too," I hoped. I began discussing this concept in many ways with whoever would listen. People I'd meet were telling me they'd discovered or been sent my article. "I was right!" This foundation, rooted in something real, allowed me to be of deeper service to the industry I lauded, coming from a place of mutual understanding and emotional equity.

Separately, I'd started making music again—producing

tracks, writing songs, and even learning guitar—eager to reclaim my original innocence and joy of the process without any added pressure. It worked. This only strengthened my perspective and introduced an ability to summon and retain new inspiration at will, preparing me to navigate the challenges of the music business with a renewed sense of purpose. By focusing internally, I started to see the positive impact of my efforts externally.

I hated reading as a kid. It wasn't until I discovered the seventh edition of Donald Passman's book *All You Need to Know About the Music Business*, the de-facto industry bible, that I read something cover-to-cover. That book served as the foundation of my early understanding of the mechanics of the music business, and subsequent versions became a guiding light throughout my career. While an incredible resource, I could've benefitted from a complementary book that focused less on the mechanics of the business and more on how to effectively maneuver and define my place within it. I also noticed a lack of books in the marketplace written from the perspective of someone actively navigating the industry in a creative capacity.

For much of my journey, I focused on trying to understand how the car operated rather than how to drive it. This book is about how to drive. It's a reflection of the core principles I've gathered throughout my career, aimed at equipping others with the tools to make better decisions that align with who they are. Whether you've just begun your journey, find yourself amidst a transition period, or are simply seeking new inspiration, this book is for you.

In Part 1, Understanding the New Music Business, we

explore the shifts that have occurred and how they impact you. Part 2, Charting Your Path, focuses on defining your unique journey and leveraging your strengths through key principles. Part 3, Balancing Passion & Profession, delves into maintaining creativity and drive while managing the challenges of turning passion into a profession. Finally, Part 4, Navigating Your Career, offers practical strategies for career transitions, developing a personal brand, and establishing a successful path in the music industry. Throughout the book, I share practical insights and real-world scenarios from my own experiences and those of other industry professionals.

Ultimately, this book is about empowering you to take control of your career, make informed decisions, and find fulfillment in your work. I invite you to dive in, embark on a journey of self-discovery and professional growth, and embrace your role as a leader of the new school—music's ultimate consumer.

Part 1: Understanding the New Music Business

There's been a shift

The music business has never been a stranger to change—whether it's been openly embraced or not is a point of contention. Yet the past decade has brought about some of the most consequential changes it's ever seen.

There's been an increased influence of financial markets on the industry. Billion-dollar valuations, publicly traded majors; is this how the 90s felt? Technology has revolutionized the business once again. AI is currently the disruptor on trial at the center of the town surrounded by skeptics and defenders alike. Layoffs and restructures have underscored the industry's turbulence. Companies like Splice, TuneCore, CD Baby, Spotify, and TikTok have completely upended the traditional music industry assembly line, decreasing the distance between producers and consumers. Independent artists are capturing an increasing number of hits without any links to a major. The power dynamics of success have become like a Rubik's Cube, constantly shifting and reconfiguring depending on the quarter or perspective in focus.

To better understand today's climate, it helps to examine how we got here. From the collapse and eventual resurgence of physical sales to the period of stagnation between the decline of downloads and the rise of streaming giants like Spotify and Apple Music, each shift has redefined how music is created, delivered, and consumed.

Back in 2015, when I first stepped into the Beverly Hills offices of Epic Records as a bright-eyed intern, the music industry was on the brink of another transformation. Fifth Harmony's "Worth It" and Omi's "Cheerleader" were blaring through the central lobby's speakers what seemed like every few minutes. And while it wasn't something I was consciously aware of, the undercurrents of change were already shaping the future.

The era of physical albums and downloads was transitioning into the nascent days of streaming. Leading indie distributors like TuneCore and CD Baby democratized digital distribution, broadening the market for companies like DistroKid, Stem, and UnitedMasters to emerge as new leaders in the space. SoundCloud was the go-to platform for independent musicians trying to make a name from their bedrooms. Blogs like *Pigeons & Planes, Fader, and 2DopeBoyz*, paired with SoundCloud and social media, were the ultimate authority for music discovery, paving the way for the eventual introduction and dominance of A&R "research" roles. Radio still held sway over which artists broke through, and record labels were still seen as an indispensable cog on an artist's path to superstardom. Just ten years prior, the business was in its early post-existential-crisis days, reeling from the drastic effects of file-sharing.

The energy was palpable. As I navigated through the hustle of label meetings, studio sessions, and artist showcases, you could sense a shift in the air. The traditional gatekeepers were losing their grip, economic implications weren't clear, and the power dynamics were beginning to change (sound familiar?). Spotify monthly listeners, displayed prominently next to an artist's name on their profile, were becoming a more important metric than Nielsen SoundScan (now Luminate), providing a real-time gauge of an artist's trajectory. Editorial playlists emerged with an impact comparable to the early days of MTV, creating a monoculture where a placement could make or break an artist's career in a world headed towards individualization. Playlist editors became the new VJs. There was an underlying sense of excitement and anxiety. But it turns out this was just the beginning of a series of shifts that would reshape the entire industry.

As we moved through the latter half of the 2010s, streaming solidified its dominance. Social media applications like Musical.ly (now TikTok), Instagram "blog" pages, and editorial playlists such as Spotify's "New Music Friday" and Apple's genre playlists became essential to a successful release strategy. Vinyl began its resurgence, carving out a niche among cool kids and audiophiles, signaling a shift back to music consumption as a tangible experience. Splice revolutionized music production by providing subscription-based royalty-free access to millions of original loops and one-shot samples, democratizing music creation and empowering millions with a laptop and a dream to create professional-grade tracks. This accessibility was both exhilarating and daunting, as it flooded the market with more music than ever before and fueled a deeper reliance on data.

Paired with the rapid effects of globalization, access to high-quality loops and samples coincided with the spread of various genres worldwide. This was particularly evident with the rise of afrobeats and Latin music, which gained international popularity thanks (in small part) to easier access to diverse sounds and collaborative opportunities. The power dynamics shifted further, with data and analytics now playing a central role in decision-making processes that were once driven purely by taste, intuition, and experience. Meanwhile, an increasing number of creative execs began exiting traditional roles in favor of entrepreneurial pursuits and newer companies, highlighting a stark contrast between the expanding creative opportunities and the industry's resistance to fully embrace these changes. The landscape was changing rapidly and staying ahead of the curve required adaptability and foresight.

At the turn of the decade (with Roddy Ricch's "The Box" going full steam), the music industry faced an unprecedented challenge: the COVID-19 pandemic. The global crisis exacerbated ongoing shifts and forced new ones. Live performances, which had long been a significant revenue stream for many artists, came to an abrupt halt as tours were canceled and venues shuttered. The collapse of IRL opportunities meant events were indefinitely postponed;

content shoots, DSP playbacks, and promo runs were scrapped, sending release plans into disarray.

In response, artists and music professionals leaned into digital platforms with renewed vigor. Artists, songwriters, and producers explored remote writing sessions, utilizing platforms like Zoom, FaceTime, Splice, and other collaborative tools to try simulating an in-person experience. TikTok began to solidify its position as the platform on the cutting edge and center of culture, largely due to their unique and highly individualized algorithm. Stuck inside with more free time than ever, it seemed like, suddenly, everyone and their mother was learning a new TikTok dance or exploring the depths of various niches tailored to their interests.

The rise of individualized algorithms further eroded the dominance of monocultural channels, creating endless opportunities for songs to gain traction and break through, regardless of their release date. Social media "influencers" gained importance in breaking songs, working artist teams and labels into a frenzy. Virtual concerts became the norm, with platforms like Instagram Live, Apple Music, Twitch, and YouTube hosting performances that brought artists directly into fans' homes. The concept of "concerts" was redefined, with interactive elements and real-time engagement becoming integral to the experience. Facing these limitations, emerging artists became increasingly creative, recording and uploading performances from unconventional locations like forests, parks, and empty public spaces. This virtual content provided a lifeline for artists and a sense of connection for fans during a time of isolation.

As the pandemic progressed, the shift towards digital accelerated. The business saw an increased reliance on social media and digital marketing to create an audience, maintain fan engagement, and promote new releases. Short-form content platforms like TikTok became even more pivotal in breaking new artists and songs, with viral trends and challenges often directly translating to increased streams and chart success. With a decline in influence of larger influencers and a growing desire for direct artist-fan interaction, artists were increasingly expected to double as content creators, deepening a sense that they must take the lead in breaking themselves. Algorithms further shaped our musical tastes, pushing us further towards individualization, reducing the importance of larger influencers and editorial playlists in determining a song's fate. The traditional methods of artist development and A&R were further disrupted as streaming data and social media metrics were solidified as primary indicators of an artist's potential.

With the pandemic in its rearview, the business finds itself facing yet another formidable force: AI. Just as streaming and social media redefined the industry's landscape over the past decade, AI has stepped into the spotlight. One of the most controversial digital developments of the 21st century, the jury's out. Tool or crutch? Friend or threat? Its influence is felt across the board—creation, distribution, discovery, and collection—transforming traditional processes at every level.

Companies are training AI music-generators on millions of pre-existing songs created and released by humans to the dismay of many artists, record, and publishing companies. One can literally input text into a prompt that will generate an entire song based on your written ideas. AI enables the creation of voice models, allowing users to replicate or craft entirely custom voices for use in their tracks. Users can now extract stems (individual instrument tracks) from two-track audio files, inspiring a new generation of DJs and producers to create limitless combinations of mashups and edits. However, this technological shift has brought about a paradoxical return to the essence of what makes music truly resonant: humanity. Its rise prompted us to re-examine music's value: is it simply an endless stream of machine-generated tracks, spoon fed to us simply to pass the time and soundtrack our short-form content? Or is it the human connection and unique perspectives that resonate most deeply?

New roles and opportunities

Ironically, in a world drowning in digital output, AI is the rod that fixed the camel's back. The good ol' days. The influx of music, along with the ease of its creation, has amplified the demand for unique perspectives. Most of the artists breaking in a big way are the ones that have been at-it for years—several albums, a few tours, dropped by a label—once overlooked by their peers. Live performances are arguably more impactful than ever, serving as a filter between consumers and artists looking to solidify their ingenuity in a world of digital noise. The short-form content revolution, coupled with the growing influences of globalization and individualism, has primed consumers for the expansion of several niche styles and genres that traditionally struggled to gain market traction.

This shift has sparked a resurgence of breakout artists and visionaries who aren't merely following trends but are instead pushing boundaries with work that reflects their personal experiences. Individual music curators have emerged as key players, offering a human-driven alternative to algorithmic recommendations and helping listeners discover music that speaks to them on a deeper level. They rekindle a sense of community that was lost during the pandemic's isolation and further fragmented by the increasing individualization of our algorithm-driven content.

The evolving landscape of the music business is not just redefining existing roles but also creating entirely new ones, offering more opportunities to participate in its evolution than ever before. Due to the rapid expansion of the business (and the effects of late-stage capitalism), many music professionals are now wearing more hats, with an increasing number of companies and individuals embracing dual roles and entrepreneurial pursuits. Whether it's navigating the nuances of digital marketing, curating playlists, crafting immersive experiences that resonate on a deeper level, or producing platforms that shape the cultural conversation, the spectrum of opportunities is continually expanding. Digital strategists, music curators, partnership leads, content creators, podcast hosts, creative producers, and artist development specialists are among the many roles that are reshaping the industry, each contributing to a dynamic and ever-evolving landscape.

Amidst these shifts and emerging opportunities, individuals are increasingly called to chart their own paths and leverage their strengths. This new era is teeming with opportunities for those who can navigate its complexities and understand the heightened value of their unique perspective. In a landscape that's constantly evolving, personal authenticity and purpose-driven decisions have become essential tools for navigating this new terrain. As the industry continues to grow and diversify, those who embrace their individuality and align their actions with a clear sense of purpose will not only find success but also contribute to shaping the future of music.

Part 2: Charting Your Path

You are the consumer

There was a point where I'd sworn off A&R roles. Scorned by industry-wide shifts away from what I considered to be the essence of A&R—intuition-based signings, artist development, and creative guidance—I'd had enough. "I went all-in on this. Do I even bring anything else to the table?" "Am I going to die on this hill?"

By then, I was years removed from my decision to trade my initial creative aspirations for more "realistic" business pursuits (like solidifying my position as a top record executive), and I decided it was time to explore other avenues if I was to continue my career in music. I never once considered another industry—not because I didn't want to, but because I felt like I had no choice. I'd set up my career to be so exclusively music-centric that I never felt I had any strengths or experiences that would translate to a successful career in another industry. I wandered through various roles in music publishing and artist management, experimenting with different genres and strategies, searching for any sense of fulfillment and belonging.

But there's a beautiful thing that happens once things hit the fan. There's a sense of surrender, accompanied by a sense of possibility. At that point, after running my own one-man show as an artist manager for a couple of years, I found myself grappling with an unexpected idea.

"Write an essay about the music business." This idea couldn't have been more random when it came to me, commanding key real estate within my mind seemingly out of nowhere. I absolutely hated writing when I was younger, and throughout high school, I was getting Ds and Cs in English class simply because I wouldn't turn in half of my assignments. I hated writing essays about books I didn't care to read. "Why would I write about something I couldn't care less about?" I spent weeks pondering over what I was going to write about. "Do I just write about the current state of the music business?" "Maybe I can write about where the business is heading." "What about A&R?" "Ah-hah! That's something I have quite a bit of perspective on." "But I haven't been working in A&R for a while nor do I agree with its current state." "Why don't I write about what I consider to be its essence?"

I didn't realize it at the time, but writing my essay *The Essence of A&R: We Are the Consumer* became a process of rediscovery—setting the standards that would later inform my return to A&R. By writing about what I believed to be its essence, I was led to a realization that extends far beyond

the world of A&R: you are the consumer. This idea first
took shape during a pivotal moment in my career, when I
recognized the disconnect between data-driven decisions
and the intuitive, human-centered approach that had origi-
nally drawn me to A&R in the first place. What began as a
principle rooted in my frustrations and experiences in A&R
revealed itself to be a universal truth for anyone in a creative
field.

Knowing you're the consumer empowers you to make
decisions that align with your own interests, not only
serving your personal goals but also contributing meaning-
fully to larger projects and ideals. It shifts your perspective,
informing every creative decision you make and serving as
the foundation for confidence in all that you do. It's about
trusting your intuition and understanding what resonates
on a deeper level. Embracing this principle removes the distance between you and the consumer, which in turn makes
you a more effective marketer and creator. You begin to
understand that if something moves you, it's likely to move
others too.

Consider Charli xcx and the runaway success of her
album *Brat*. By recognizing that she's the consumer—a
chronically online millennial, deeply embedded in internet
culture, and a lover of campy pop music—she was able to
define her audience with precision and capture the zeitgeist.
This authenticity shines through in her work, resonating
with others who share her perspective. By knowing what
she sought as a consumer, Charli tapped into a broader
audience that craves the same things.

This understanding helps you craft work that is not

only authentic but also deeply connected to the audience you aim to reach. By embodying this principle, you start to surround yourself with influences, ideas, and collaborators that align with your vision. You attract what you resonate with, and that synergy—a true reflection of your own taste and values—can elevate your work to new heights.

"What would need to happen for me to love this?"

Find your angle and remain curious

We all know the importance of knowing our strengths—but what if you're not sure what they are? It wasn't until relatively recently that I started to form a more comprehensive understanding of my strengths. Understanding our strengths helps us develop the interests and skill sets that shape our confidence, making us more effective collaborators and expanding our possibilities.

If everyone's always passing you the aux, there's a good chance you have a great ear. If you're always coming up with creative ways for people to work together, it's likely you're a partnerships wiz. The best way to uncover your strengths is by observing the patterns in your life that align with your natural interests and inclinations. Your path is like a geometric angle; the starting point sets your direction. For years, I knew I was good at certain things, but I struggled to fully own them as strengths—partly because I kept comparing myself to others, and partly because I didn't realize that strengths aren't fully formed from the start. They're refined and expanded through curiosity.

It's when you start asking questions, taking risks, and stepping outside your routine that you really start to uncover what you're capable of. Curiosity isn't just about exploring new things—it's about digging deeper into what already interests you while regularly challenging your beliefs. Your beliefs should constantly be put to the test. The ones worth holding onto will continue to pass, and the others will dissipate, leaving room for new ones to form. This allows you to find new ways of applying your skills and lets your strengths evolve naturally.

Take my own journey as an example. My obsession with music and curiosity led me from DJing to making music, then into A&R, which seemed like the most natural path given my skills at the time. But I didn't stop there—I explored music publishing and artist management, before eventually writing an essay that brought me back to A&R and making music. If I hadn't remained curious and open, I wouldn't have expanded my skill sets or seized new opportunities. When you're willing to remain curious, you're not just sticking to the path you've set—you're expanding it, opening new directions and opportunities that you never saw coming.

Discover your sense of urgency

Hesitation can be the difference between life and death in the music business. Yet living each moment like it's your last sparks the kind of inspired actions that sustain and define careers. Let's face it: regardless of its intricacies, the music industry is one of the most desirable professions in the world. Millions of passionate individuals would kill for an opportunity to get paid to listen, create, promote, and talk about music all day. The competition is fierce, as there's never been more talent in queue waiting for their chance to take your spot. So, what sets you apart? Urgency. Urgency points to a reverence that drives you to act decisively, seize opportunities as they come, and stay ahead in an industry that often rewards those who move first. It enables creativity. Urgency becomes the catalyst, fueling a relentless pursuit of greatness and innovation.

I like to characterize my sense of urgency as a burning desire often followed by resistance. It's a feeling of insistence that permeates your entire being and won't diminish until you're forced into action (best remedy I've found for the plight of neurodivergence). Without a sense of urgency, doubt creeps in, and an idle mind becomes the breeding ground for complacency, causing overall performance to suffer and leaving great ideas unexecuted. Moving quickly forces you to act on your inspiration, preventing complacency. But it isn't just about speed; it's about recognizing when you need to push yourself or projects beyond your comfort zone to take advantage of inspiration strikes and stay ahead of the curve. Growth often comes from our moments of greatest discomfort, where we embrace resistance. When you follow the resistance, you're led along a path of overcoming inertia, building momentum that propels you forward.

There's a story that lives rent-free in my head—perfectly capturing the essence of urgency and its importance. Legend has it that Michael Jackson, upon receiving bursts of inspiration, would frantically act on those ideas, partially driven by the fear that Prince would beat him to it. This sense of urgency is what kept Michael ahead of the curve, always striving for excellence.

Similarly, I witnessed firsthand while on his management team how 24kGoldn exemplified this principle, changing the game entirely. He was determined to break through. He recognized the unique power of short-form content before most artists did. Nowadays, developing artists are all but expected to lead their own short-form content strategies, but at the dawn of TikTok's reign, most teams focused on paying influencers to promote their music. Goldn, alongside a brilliant digital strategist named Michael Uy, understood that by creating and posting content himself, he could directly engage with his audience. He invited influencers to his shows, collaborated with them on TikTok, and quickly built a community. His ability to move quickly and harness the platform's potential not only set him apart but also allowed him to stay ahead of trends and pave his own way forward in the business. The culmination of his efforts was a #1 on the *Billboard* Hot 100 for his song "Mood (featuring Iann Dior)," which spent eight non-consecutive weeks at the summit.

A sense of urgency is about acting with intention, pushing through resistance, and continuously striving for growth. This mindset doesn't just propel you forward—it combats complacency, enabling creativity and inspiring those around you to do the same. As you channel this drive, it naturally leads to innovation, empowering yourself and others, and fostering a community built on shared momentum and a commitment to continuous improvement.

Empower yourself

Never, and I mean *never*, confuse your identity with your role. Relying on others for your empowerment is one of the worst mistakes you can make in the 21st-century music business. This is for a couple of reasons, the first being that technology has made it so you don't have to, and the second being that you're setting yourself up for disappointment. With a constant shifting of power dynamics, audience trends, politics, layoffs, and other economic factors, this business is unpredictable.

The music industry sometimes feels like one big Halloween party where everyone is dressed as ghosts. One day, you're sure it's there and an agreement's been reached. The next day, you're chasing shadows wondering what could've happened. Artists often face this lesson the hard way upon chasing and relying on deals that directly place their fate in the hands of others. "If only I could get x, I could make xyz." Execs face this when they hinge everything upon a specific job, only to get shown the door or left on read (this literally just happened to me, as I write this book). In such a volatile environment, relying on others is a risk you can't afford. Instead, why not create your own opportunities? Waiting for someone else to hand you an opportunity, give you a job, or provide the resources you need is a zero-sum game, and focusing so much on disputing its rulebook leads nowhere.

Here's the thing: at no point in time has the average individual had more access to creative resources and opportunities than now. The beauty of self-empowerment is that it not only safeguards you against the industry's uncertainties but also opens a world of possibilities. Why wait for others when you can create value for yourself? The most fulfilling achievements come from leaning into what you can control. It's about gathering your own tools, trusting your instincts, and seeing what you're meant to create.

Creation can assume many forms from this perspective. A creative work: "What can I make, and what do I need to make it?" A community: "Who may I connect with that shares similar interests?" An opportunity: "Where can I apply my skills to create value?" When you empower yourself, you discover new skills, build a community that follows you where you go, and end up creating the unique perspective that others will seek from you anyway. It's a process that not only builds resilience but also helps you carve out a path that is uniquely yours.

As you continue to empower yourself, you'll find that

the value you create becomes your foundation. But there's another crucial step to ensure your efforts aren't just momentary flashes but enduring legacies: ownership. Empowerment is about taking charge of your journey, but ownership is what secures your place on the map.

Own something, always

When I left my role at Epic Records to pursue an opportunity at Pulse, Paul Pontius, one of Epic's senior A&R executives offered me one of the best pieces of wisdom I've received as a parting gift; "own something, always." "Whether it's A&R points or something else, it will allow you to build real wealth and go as far in this business as you'd like." I didn't realize it at the time, but boy was he right. In a business as dynamic as the music industry, ownership is your anchor. It's what allows you to build something that lasts, something you control, and ultimately, something that defines your identity. It becomes your cushion when you're inevitably fired for various reasons in or out of your control (par for the course). Whether it's your music, your brand, or even your ideas, owning something means you have a stake in your success and the freedom to navigate your path as you see fit.

Fresh off working on the management teams of 24kGoldn and Rich the Kid, I ended up using the first year of the pandemic as a window to launch my own artist development company, specializing in management and consulting services. Business aside, it was a declaration of independence. I was free! I'd spent the preceding few years in a constant pursuit of various jobs—eager to make an impact yet simultaneously confusing my worth with my title. This was in direct contrast with my childhood, where I was always creating brands and companies surrounding my musical pursuits. The first one (naturally) was a DJ service. Once I began producing artists, there was (obviously) a fledging record label. At one point there was even a "lifestyle" streetwear brand.

That entrepreneurial spirit is what initially drove me into the music industry. Running your own show, even while working full-time within a corporate structure, fosters a sense of entrepreneurship and freedom that's invaluable. The mindset of "eating what you kill" becomes more than just a survival tactic—it becomes a source of confidence and inspiration.

Over time, this venture can shift in focus, sometimes even becoming your primary source of income or your main professional focus. Generating an income stream you can control through these endeavors reduces your dependency on any single job, alleviating the desperation that often comes with job insecurity. That's why so many successful music executives and creatives come from money. Financial independence is crucial in an industry as unpredictable as music, as it allows you to pursue opportunities that align with your values and passions, ultimately enhancing job satisfaction and career longevity. This approach pushes you to be more resourceful and brings a sense of autonomy and self-reliance into every project you touch, allowing you to lead with purpose and conviction in any role.

Ownership isn't just a safety net; it's a statement of intent. It's about taking control of your career and ensuring that you have something that is yours, no matter what. When you own something, whether it's a piece of music, a book, a platform, a brand, or a business, you create lasting value that can withstand the inevitable tides of the music business. Owning something becomes your footing when everything else around you shifts. Let that ownership be the cornerstone of your long-term success.

Maintain open borders

It's easy to fall into the trap of rigidly defining your role—I've been there. Early in my career, I started to believe that to advance, I needed to specialize in a specific role with a tightly focused skillset. I've come to refer to this as "closing your borders." And the more I defined those borders, the more I convinced myself that success was black and white—an idea that conflicted with my childhood. Back then, I didn't give a damn about boundaries—my creativity steered the ship. Yet, as I got older, I kept hearing the old trope: "A jack of all trades is a master of none." Turns out the adults completely missed the latter half of Shakespeare's quote: "A jack of all trades is a master of none, *but oftentimes better than a master of one.*" My inner child was correct.

Politics aside, closed borders don't just keep things out—they keep you in. For years, I confined my identity within these self-imposed borders, thinking that staying in my lane was the key to success. It wasn't. It took me nearly a decade to realize that my most valuable contributions come when I allow myself to step beyond those boundaries. The real key was opening those borders—not just for others, but for myself.

About a decade ago as I began interning at Epic, I was separately working with a talented rapper from Long Beach named King Pen on an LP called *Momentum*. I would drive over a hundred miles a day from Valencia going between the studio in Long Beach and college in Hollywood. I produced most of the tracks, oversaw the recording process, mixed the records, designed the artwork, and performed as his official DJ. At the time, a big goal was to get King Pen signed, but we ended up releasing the project independently through TuneCore. My focus shifted toward my executive aspirations, and I entered a self-imposed period of writer's block and indefinitely retired my identity as a creative.

Thankfully, King Pen kept pushing our music, and in 2018, we licensed the project to a sync licensing company to find ways to exploit our works in visual media. Fast forward to 2024, when I was notified a song from *Momentum* was placed in a critically acclaimed A24 feature film called *A Different Man.* Saying I was shocked would be a gross mischaracterization. This was a song I produced nearly a decade ago, now featured in a major motion picture by arguably the most reputable studio in the world. How about that? I had set aside my creative identity to focus on being an executive, believing I had to fit into a specific mold. But that song wouldn't be in an A24 film today if I hadn't kept a door open to my creative side, even when it wasn't my primary focus. By doing so, I allowed a decade-old piece of work to find new life, reminding me that growth often comes from the places we least expect.

My experiences at Def Jam with Breez Kennedy, his manager Damon "Dee" Gomes, and Genia have further illustrated the importance of keeping our roles fluid. They've each inspired me in ways that go beyond expression. While Dee's title is manager, his involvement goes outside the traditional scope as he co-writes many of Breez's songs—a reflection of his own background as an artist. My own journey, rooted in production, songwriting, and DJing, brings another layer to my A&R work, allowing us to push boundaries and explore new ideas together. And beyond developing her new sound, Genia and I incessantly brainstorm fresh content ideas to help her connect more deeply with her audience. These are superpowers. This flexibility doesn't blur the lines to the point of chaos; rather, it enhances our collaboration, deepening our collective investment in the creative process. Allowing others to cross borders while maintaining clear responsibilities is key.

In an industry where new roles constantly emerge, this approach ensures that essential tasks don't get lost or slip through the cracks. By keeping our borders open, we've created an environment where each person's full range of skills enriches the work, making it more inspired and rewarding. It's a reminder that titles don't define the limits of our contributions, and maybe in your own journey, there's an opportunity to push those borders a little wider and discover just how much more you can achieve.

Sustain your drive through hobbies

Working in the music business can feel like you're driving toward a moving destination in a broken-down vehicle perpetually on E, no matter how often you stop for gas. The journey is exhausting, and your one sliver of hope is that maybe, just maybe, you'll reach this elusive target without totaling the car. "Maybe I'll even find a McDonalds with a working ice cream machine along the way." I know this journey all too well... but this isn't simply "how it is." It doesn't have to be this way; in fact, it shouldn't be. What if, with a quick shift in perspective, the journey becomes a road trip instead?

Consumers, by nature, are driven by their hobbies, much like the way a road trip's magic lies in the unexpected detours and simple joy of exploring new things. In creative industries like the music business, it's often our initial hobbies that inspire the journey. But when our passion becomes our profession, it can create a callous indifference. Hobbies offer that original sense of adventure, keeping you in a mindset of exploration and delight, which in turn fuels your passion and sustains your momentum. They provide the perfect counterbalance to the pressures of the business—a way to refuel your creative tank and keep your passion alive. Ultimately, it's these moments of connection that remind us why we chose this path in the first place, helping us to maintain the passion and creativity necessary to navigate the industry's challenges. By embracing hobbies, you allow yourself to step outside the relentless pursuit of success, refresh your perspective, and reconnect with the simple pleasures that initially drew you to the road.

For me, this shift in perspective began after I fell out of love with music and found solace in nature. The sounds of birds singing, leaves rustling, and even distant human chatter started to resonate with me in ways I had never noticed before. One time, I vividly remember standing on the edge of Little Dume Beach in Malibu with my now-fiancée Sheeva, lost in the stillness of the evening, listening to the tide crash against the rocks in the cove below. In that moment, it felt like we were part of a live symphony at the Hollywood Bowl, with each sound playing its part in perfect harmony. The stillness was remarkable. The silence between each sound was almost addicting, deepening my ear and inviting me to listen carefully to the subtle details around me. A renewed sense of hearing through these types of experiences gradually brought me back to music.

After a lifetime consumed by creating and organizing

noise, the irony of finding so much joy in silence and the mundane isn't lost on me. Weekly, I sought out different landscapes, frequenting places like Bluff Cove in Palos Verdes or somewhere in Malibu, eager for reprieve from the hum of the city. Camping (all throughout California) became my favorite pastime, yet with time I found that the trips to the campsites—the cafes, the diners, the thrift stores, and even the car rides—all held as much weight in my enjoyment as the actual camping.

When I returned to creating music, I had rediscovered the joy of creation—my old passion reignited. But this time I knew how to keep it alive. Like with nature, learning guitar has become a personal journey, a way to deepen the connection with music that once felt out of reach. I realized the destination is fleeting, but the random stops along the way, each one offering its own kind of fuel, keep me going. It's these moments of renewal that keep the journey alive, ensuring that the road ahead remains free of doom and full of possibility.

Fix the bridge for others to cross

The music industry, like any other, is built on the shoulders of those who came before us, but its evolution often leaves cracks in the foundation that demand attention. It's like an old bridge, rattled by quakes and exposing new vulnerabilities. If these gaps persist, they'll undermine the industry's ability to prosper. Whether it's retracting the bounds of creativity, advocating for songwriters, or taking chances on new talent, these gaps aren't mere challenges—they're opportunities to reinforce the path forward and shape the future. It's not enough to simply cross the bridge ourselves; we must also ensure it's strong enough for others to follow.

As individualism hastens the demise of community, some artists and execs alike are realizing that while progress may begin in isolation, it's truly driven by the power of community. We need more artists and creatives collaborating for the sake of collaboration, without letting business disrupt the process. Industry-shaping movements start with a collective of like-minded individuals—artists, creatives, consumers—who share a common vision. Those passionate about better music, for example, have a vested interest in fixing songwriter economics. Or perhaps you endured an experience that inspires a new project. Being vulnerable and sharing the gamut of your experiences with others helps you create lasting connections and deepen your sense of community. These communities become collaborative hubs and incubators for innovation, serving as centers that eventually build a collective force. Each member brings something unique to the table, pushing one another to break boundaries and chart new territories. But as individuals are propelled forward and assume greater roles, it's vital to pull others along, ensuring the momentum continues. This collective effort fortifies the entire business, securing it with fresh ideas and perspectives.

If you've met me, it's highly likely you've heard me mention Chris Anokute at some point or two. Chris, an A&R executive I met during my internship at Epic Records, is the one who brought me in full-time as his A&R assistant. He gave me my first real shot and continued to pass the ball. Simply put, I'm not sure where I'd be in this business without his early belief and mentorship. If my internship opened the door to the business, Chris didn't just hold it open—he yanked me through and made sure I was fed. He saw something in me that others didn't and decided to take a chance on my talent. Chris encouraged my ideas, taught me the business, and threw me straight into the fire, allowing me to meet key people and quickly gain hands-on experience with A-list artists. Once I proved myself, he even introduced me to Tinashe and her team—the first major artist for whom I was fortunate to A&R while still an assistant. He refused to call me his assistant, always referring to me as a "star" in every conversation, whether internal or external. It was all huge for me, because he was one of the first people—outside of my parents and sister—that had acknowledged the potential I saw in myself. Beyond that, he opened his network, a move that quickly jumpstarted my career and bolstered my credibility within the industry.

In addition to Chris, there were other execs who took me under their wing and embraced my perspective. Zoe Young was responsible for my first ever A&R credit—French Montana's album *Jungle Rules* that produced the RIAA diamond-certified single, "Unforgettable (featuring Swae Lee)." She also introduced me to Rich the Kid, who I ended up signing to Pulse and subsequently managing.

Prior to that, I learned from another brilliant A&R executive named Sickamore. Sick had an enigmatic approach that helped him deliver, prioritizing artistic connection and creative fluidity over label politics. At the start of my internship, he was finishing both Travis Scott's critically and commercially acclaimed *Birds in the Trap Sing McKnight* and YG's *My Krazy Life*. I remember sitting in his office one day, chatting about a college course I was taking called Transmedia Design. This class was about telling consistent stories throughout different forms of media. Sick took a special interest in my outlook from this class and tasked me with analyzing the storytelling of popular concept albums.

Within a week of sharing the breakdowns (for reasons that still amaze me), he ended up inviting me to join him and YG in a private studio session at Snoop Dogg's spot in Long Beach, where I was tasked with finding and filling the narrative gaps for *Still Brazy*. As an LA native, this was surreal. Here I was, an intern with a musical hoop dream, sitting in a studio with one of my favorite artists at the time, explaining to *him* how to make his project stronger.

The concept of paying it forward was ingrained in me from the onset of my career—though, honestly? For a while, I didn't feel like I had anything of value to share. I eventually realized this feeling stemmed from not having gone through the necessary experiences that would later impart wisdom and prompt my desire to give back. Earlier this year, I was the keynote speaker at a showcase for upcoming musicians and professionals, many eager to find their footing in the business. As we spoke, memories of when I was just starting out came rushing back. I couldn't believe I was the one on the other side, the one being asked the questions. I felt like Dre from *Brown Sugar*. I'd previously sat on panels before my industry contemporaries, but this was much more fulfilling. Their passion was inspiring, and their questions reminded me of the challenges I faced and the lessons I had to learn along the way. Seeing their drive and thirst for knowledge made me realize that the experiences I've gathered could maybe provide valuable perspective for others too.

Community and mentorship are the legacies we leave behind, shaping the industry for future generations. When you find yourself in a position to connect or uplift, remember: the reach of your influence extends far beyond the immediate. By bringing others along, you're not only aiding their growth but also enhancing your own. We must ensure that the bridges we cross today are fortified for those who will follow, enabling them to chart new paths and build upon the foundations we've laid. In doing so, we foster a resilient, innovative music business that thrives on collective progress and shared success.

Part 3: Balancing Passion & Profession

Turning passion into profession

Passion lies in the heart of consumerism, fueling its engine. It's the fire that ignites our interests and drives us to dive deeper into what we enjoy. Think about it—our first steps are always as consumers. Tunji Balogun, now Chairman and CEO of Def Jam, cut his teeth as an artist, giving him the rare ability to relate to and understand their journey firsthand. It starts with a simple interest—"I think I like movies." (Watches more movies.) That interest evolves into an obsession—"I love movies. Who made them?" (Starts researching filmmakers.) And, naturally, obsessions often come with an innate desire to get closer to the source—"I could do that!" (Makes first short film, updates social media bio.) It's all fun and games—until you start making money from it. At first, it's incredible. "Wow, I can't believe I'm actually getting paid for this." You're a mix of excited, inspired, surprised, and maybe a little bit conflicted, especially considering all the resistance and criticism you might've faced from peers or even family about needing a "backup plan." "Entertainment is a cutthroat business, and there's no money in it unless you're related to someone or get lucky." But when that passion becomes your profession, everything changes.

Joy and spontaneity, once the pillars that effortlessly upheld your passion, begin to crumble under the weight of anxiety, as your passion meets the pressures of work, deadlines, and financial expectations. This shift is both exhilarating and challenging, as the joy you once felt now comes with a weight you never expected—responsibility. Once you taste success, you want to repeat it. You retrace your steps, analyzing every move that "got you" here. You seek input or guidance from "trusted" sources, typically those who have successfully done what you're trying to do. You start comparing your path with others. Your brain forms systems around that passion, mistakenly believing structure will replicate or surpass that initial success. It's a tug-of-war between the part of you that fell in love with the craft and the part that knows the stakes have changed. The joy is still there, but it's confined within the structure of expectation, each side pulling you in different directions. But that's where we falter—because passion and creativity aren't meant to be contained. They exist outside of any framework.

So how do you keep the passion alive when the stakes are higher than ever? *Freedom*. You need a passion (or three) that remains untouched by the demands of your profession, freeing your creativity and preserving your original spark—

the spark that first ignited your love for the craft, your most valuable asset. Protect it, nurture it, and let it fuel your growth. The business might demand structure, but your passion thrives in freedom. Balance is the key—let your profession sharpen your skills, but let your passion keep you inspired. This delicate balance is what will keep you creative, driven, and happy, no matter how high the stakes become.

Maintaining creativity and drive

When the allure of DJing began to wear off, I realized I
needed more. It had always been about the joy of moving
people through music. I started as a curious consumer,
finding and mixing records, and almost immediately, I
found myself DJing paid events most weekends. Those early
experiences taught me music could be more than a hobby;
it was something I could build a career around. My passion
and profession were entwined from the jump. But by the
time I got to high school, the thrill of DJing had started
to fade into routine. I'd DJed over a hundred events by my
junior year. I still loved music, but I craved a new challenge—something that would reignite the spark and push
me beyond what I already knew.

That's when producing music caught my interest. DJing
had quickly shifted from hobby to profession, so producing

became a new, deeper extension of that DJ mindset, adding new layers to my work. It felt like the next step in my creative journey—moving beyond selecting and mixing tracks to creating the songs that could evoke those same emotions. As a DJ, I'd learned what moves an audience, observing crowd reactions in real-time and adapting my choices based on the energy of the room. Producing took that understanding further, deepening my grasp of what makes a song truly compelling. I started with remixes and mashups, which then evolved into composing original tracks, recording, and producing artists. Since I wasn't getting paid for this, it kept music fun, pressure free. It was no longer just a means to an end, which kept burnout at bay.

Then, as I moved into A&R, my perspective widened again. It wasn't just about songs anymore; it became about identifying the types of artists who bring songs to life. A&R added another layer of creation—helping artists develop their unique sounds based on what I felt was missing from the marketplace. It was about finding, shaping, and guiding the artists who could capture the feeling of the songs that once lit me up as a DJ. A&R became another way to connect with the music that had always been my passion, but with the added excitement of shaping its future direction. But as I became more entrenched in my career as an executive, I faced a new dilemma: I had gone all-in on my professional pursuits, leaving no room for hobbies, let alone ones related to my profession. This all-or-nothing approach exhausted my creativity, which diminished my potential. I realized that I needed to recreate a similar balance to what I had when I was younger—a balance that kept me energized and inspired.

I began carving out time for creativity beyond my work—writing songs, think pieces, creating tracks again, learning guitar, and just playing around with ideas, simply for the joy of it. These pursuits weren't weighed down by deadlines or the pressure to succeed; they were just for me. In doing so, I found that familiar spark reignited. Maintaining this balance is essential—not just for me, but for anyone who wants to preserve their energy in an industry that never stops demanding.

Part 4: Navigating Your Career

We all start somewhere

Usually, it begins with a potent cocktail of passion, doubt, and a touch of wild ambition. You're driven (responsibly) by something you can't quite pin, eager to find your place in a landscape that feels both intoxicating and dispiriting. You arrive at the scene, but there's a line around the block. With its grandeur, the music business is often portrayed as an elusive club, a pipe dream with limited spots, seemingly reserved for superstars and nepo-babies. It's alluring, unpredictable, and always *just* out of reach. You wonder if you're making the right moves or if anyone even notices your efforts. But here's the truth: while the velvet ropes might seem impenetrable, the doors do open—for those who keep showing up. We all start somewhere, often with little more than a feeling that we belong, guided by intuition and the determination to see it through.

Starting out is never easy. The music business, like any creative field, is riddled with uncertainty. Most in this industry, from artists to execs, began at the bottom, not knowing where they'd end up. The key is to keep going, keep learning, and keep finding new ways to show up. The rules change constantly, and you're never certain if the club you're waiting to enter will even open next week. This is an industry where everyone has an opinion (including those outside it) and thinks theirs is the correct one. Overcoming your own doubts while reconciling the concerns of others is like a rite of passage. You'll hear a hundred different pieces of advice, often contradicting each other. One minute, you're told to focus on perfecting your craft; the next, it's about having a plan B. Some say it's about who you know, others say there are no gatekeepers. "Find someone to hire you." "It's better to create your own thing." It's enough to make your head spin. The reality is: all of it is true. In this business, no two paths are the same. Every success story you've heard began with someone standing exactly where you are now—wondering how to take that first step or if their next move will be the right one. There's no secret formula. What works for one may not work for another.

But that's exactly why your path is yours to define. Be willing to learn, adapt, and keep moving, even when the way forward isn't clear. The good news? There are more ways than ever to get into the music business. Once a tight-knit circle, there are new spots opening up all the time for those who dare to try. While there may be no secret passcode, there are steps you can take to move past the velvet ropes—staking your claim and making your mark.

Annabelle Kline-Zilles began by simply sharing her love for music—curating playlists, DJing events, and posting about artists she loves on social media. She didn't follow a blueprint; she followed her instincts with a relentless drive to connect people through music. That passion drew people in. Today, she's not just a sought-after music curator, DJ, and content creator but the founder of her own community that champions emerging artists and hosts live events. What started as a passion project exploring her tastes evolved into a platform called *That Good Sh*t* that amplifies voices and fosters creativity, proving there are countless ways to make an impact when you have the guts to go after what excites you.

Pinpoint your passion; for me, it was creating the soundtrack of pop culture, driven by the thrill of making and releasing music. What genuinely excites you about the music business? Is it the creative process? The business side? Building relationships with artists? Or perhaps you've just always loved putting your friends on to new music. Knowing "why" is your North Star, guiding you through moments of doubt and keeping you centered when the landscape shifts.

From there, just put yourself out there. It helps to know someone, but contrary to popular belief, it's not necessary (I didn't). There's never been more access to resources or potential contacts than now. Release your songs, share content that genuinely reflects your passion, and see where it takes you. Start with people who are doing what interests you. I wish I'd known earlier that there's nothing to fear—most of us are winging it, and you'd be surprised how many are willing to help if approached with courtesy and value. Master the cold DM or email—an underrated skill you'll continue to develop throughout your career. Rejection is an inevitable part of the journey, a challenge that drives growth. The worst that can happen is you don't get a reply, and the best? It could open a door to an opportunity you never imagined. Each "no" builds resilience, and each "yes" opens doors, shaping you into the person who reaches their goals and redefines what's possible.

Early on, I put too much emphasis on networking "up," thinking I had to reach for those ahead of me to succeed. This backfired, creating a hierarchy in my mind that placed everyone above me and restricted my audacity. The truth is the best way to build a network is to level the playing field, treating every interaction like it matters—because it does. Look around. Some of the most valuable relationships you'll build are with peers, the ones who are just as hungry and clueless as you are. The people you come up with are the ones who end up running things, aiding your longevity. Everyone in this business has a story, a unique perspective, and something to offer. Approach every conversation with genuine curiosity. Discover what you can give. Whether you're talking to a fellow newcomer or an industry vet, treat everyone with the same respect and consideration. The ones you overlook today could be your collaborators, champions, or even your bosses tomorrow.

It's never about having all the answers from day one. It's about knowing what drives you and being open to the unpredictable nature of this business. Sometimes, the best opportunities come from the most unexpected places, and the smallest gestures—those simple, instinctive moves driven by passion—often lead to the strongest connections. Every interaction, no matter how minor it seems, could be what ushers your way forward or brings you closer to the people who will help you get there.

Handling transitions

In today's music business, complacency is the kiss of death. It used to be that one could find their way into a building and ride out into the sunset collecting paychecks and benefits, fate secured by golden parachute clauses and limited distribution channels. Companies wielded more power, but there was a baseline of loyalty. The great part about this was that it allowed people to focus on their craft without the constant fear of instability, which created more specialists. But it also created a perfect breeding ground for the very complacency that's long riddled the business. Now, with corporate loyalty dwindling and an industry earmarked by continuous change, playing it safe is the quickest way to be left behind.

Change is always difficult, but transitions don't have to be negative. Trust me, I get the difficulties—bills piling up, your phone stops ringing, people you thought were friends setting you aside for those in better positions—it's one of the most disheartening experiences you'll go through. But whether you're an executive or an artist, relying on a single job or company for long-term security is increasingly unrealistic. Companies are no longer bastions of loyalty, and expecting them to be will only set you up for disappointment. Artists must now navigate a landscape of constant change, from evolving trends to shifting roles and the ever-demanding audience. In this climate, success favors those who remain versatile, committed to continuous learning, and ready to pivot when necessary. You should always consider yourself amidst a transition; it keeps you on your toes and actively engaged with your career. At worst, it'll maintain your sense of urgency. At best, you'll seize an exciting opportunity without the desperation that comes with forced instability—like a job loss. Stars are meant to go where they align. Transitions are opportunities to realign your path and find new ways to add value.

To successfully maneuver this landscape, you must deliver on multiple fronts. Though today's industry is increasingly dictated by financial pressures over individual merit, it also provides the freedom and resources to chart your own path. Your stability comes from your ability to connect, innovate, and reinvent yourself.

- **Build genuine communities:** Invest in building real, supportive communities that will follow you wherever you go. These aren't just professional networks but circles of trust to lean on during times of uncertainty. Reach out to your network, not just when you need something, but as a way of maintaining genuine relationships. These are the people who offer support, guidance, and opportunities during difficult transitions.

- **Practice vulnerability:** Be open and honest about what you're going through. Many people, myself included, have missed the element of vulnerability when reaching out to their networks. Being candid about your experiences, challenges, and aspirations deepens emotional connections and fosters a genuine investment in your success. Remember, most people are inherently good and willing to help—they just need to know you at your essence. Lower your guard, be transparent, and show why helping you is worth their time and effort.

- **Reflect and reframe your experiences:** Use transitions as a time to reflect on where you've added value in the past. Consider how you can recontextualize these experiences to demonstrate your unique perspective and strengths. Think about how potential employers or collaborators can benefit from the gamut of what you bring to the table. This reflection will help you craft a narrative that makes you stand out, even when you're between roles.

- **Find purpose in helping others:** Economic pressures during transitions can be intense, but there's power in using this time to help others who are in a similar position. Whether it's volunteering for a charitable organization, offering your expertise to peers, or collaborating on new projects, these actions will help you feel more grounded and build confidence. They often open new doors you might not have considered.

- **Explore new passions and ventures:** Transitions are the perfect time to explore hobbies or side projects that could eventually turn into new income streams or even a new career direction. Use these periods to cultivate skills that you might not have had time for previously, and to discover new interests that can keep your creative energy alive and open up unexpected opportunities.

Take Ray Daniels for example. Ray built his career on two parallel tracks: as a manager developing a top songwriter (Theron Thomas, 2024's GRAMMY songwriter of the year) and as a major label A&R executive. He was flourishing in both roles, using his expertise to shape talent and navigate the intricacies of the music business. After the killing of George Floyd, Ray was inspired to use his voice for social justice, penning an open letter (published by *Billboard*) about his experiences as a Black music executive. I remember when it was published—it was honest, bold, and everyone was talking about it. When his contract was up, it wasn't renewed. Losing the steady paycheck, benefits, and a senior executive title—one that often carries more weight in this industry than it should—was certainly a blow. But instead of letting himself be sidelined, Ray had discovered his voice and doubled down on it.

He started a podcast called *The Gaud Show*, a platform sharing his insights and advocating for a better music business, taking control of his own narrative. Rather than wait for someone else to give him a platform, he created his own. One that wasn't tied to any specific title or company. Now, he's not only a key voice in the music business but also a significant figure in Black culture. His experiences and perspective became a launchpad for a platform that follows him wherever he goes. In doing so, he's carved out a space for himself that's arguably more influential than many of the record label execs he used to work for. He took matters into his own hands, and now his impact reaches far beyond what any job title ever could.

Transitions can be daunting, but they're also powerful opportunities to redefine your narrative. Don't wait for permission or a title to validate your worth. Embrace change, amplify your voice, and carve out a space that only you can fill.

Developing a personal brand

"What hill am I willing to die on?"—it's a question at the heart of who you are and what you stand for. It's standing on business. It's the foundation for everything you say, create, and represent. It's not about catchy slogans or flashy aesthetics, nor is it designed to make you liked by everyone. Your brand is built on beliefs and values, a commitment to speaking your truth and centering your perspective in everything you do. Consistency is the backbone of trust, and the trust you'll build is what turns a brand from something fleeting into something lasting. What do you refuse to compromise on, no matter the circumstances? When you own your narrative this deeply, people won't have to wonder what you represent—they'll know.

Your personal brand is the lens through which you view every decision and opportunity. Without this clarity you're a fish without an eye. "Why can't I see? What should I do?" A clear brand is how you know what does and doesn't align with the core of who you are. It's what draws you to likeminded individuals with complementary perspectives. It becomes a powerful tool for filtering out distractions and staying focused on what matters most. Every word you speak, every song you release, every piece of content you create, and every deal you make reflects what you believe in, ensuring there's never a doubt about where you stand. You'd be challenged to name an artist, creative, or exec that's broken big that doesn't have a clear and recognizable brand. And beyond just putting on a show—you're showing up.

They say, "Imitation is the biggest form of flattery," but to be clear, that only applies to those being copied, not the ones interested in building an impactful brand. Between an influx of run-of-the-mill AI-generated content and the glorification of individualized facades, personal brands have an increased efficacy and importance. People just want something real. Yes, it's possible to replicate some success off the heels of someone else's brand, but don't get it twisted; there's a ceiling when you're limited by the bounds of another's perspective, shaped by their own experiences. People are drawn to authenticity, not imitation. Your brand should look and feel like you or the character you're creating: distinct, recognizable, and aligned with your values. Make your brand so consistent that people think of you the moment they hear certain words, see certain colors, or feel certain vibes.

When you're clear on what you stand for, everything else—personal style, tone, visuals—falls into place naturally.

The aesthetics of your brand are just the outward expression of your inner convictions. Don't get caught up chasing trends or trying to fit into what's popular; focus on what feels right to you. The clearer you are, the easier it is for others to understand you, and when you fully embrace who you are, the world takes notice. Your brand is beyond what you create—it's how you consume the world around you. And as I've found, it's a truth that's shaped everything I stand for.

Conclusion

The road ahead is yours to navigate—no maps, no guarantees, just the compass you build from what excites you and what you stand for. I wasn't always certain how to trust my own compass. There were times I felt completely lost, doubting if I'd ever find my way. But those moments taught me that the greatest clarity comes from within. Rather than an industry manual, I hope this book serves as a reminder that your greatest assets are your perspective, your choices, and your commitment to your own journey. I hope it's a book you can flip open to any page and find something that sparks inspiration, regardless of where you find yourself on your journey. Remember, no one else gets to define you or your path. Trust your compass, drive with purpose, and confidently chart the path that feels right to you. Because at the end of the day, *you* are the consumer.

Acknowledgments

I'm deeply grateful for everyone who has supported, inspired, and guided me on this journey.

To Sheeva, Mama, Daddy, Sarah, and Carol—your love, belief, and unwavering support have been the foundation of my strength and made all of this possible.

To the Khoshkish family and Sheeva's closest friends—thank you for welcoming me with open arms and supporting us on this journey together.

To my closest friends from the start of my "professional" career at Epic Records: Charles Burks, Kate Loesch, Brooke Marcimo, and Jamie Crawford-Walker—you have been a beacon of inspiration throughout the tides of this business, and your friendship and belief in me have been invaluable.

To Andrew Brochetti, Courtney Kloné, Dillon Ceglio,

and Susie Dunner—your unwavering support and encouragement have been a steady anchor.

With immense gratitude to my mentor turned brother, Chris Anokute, who was the first to validate my place in this industry. You taught me the power of my perspective and gave me the opportunity to shine. Your belief in me continues to inspire my journey.

To my other mentors, Zoe Young, Sickamore, Paul Pontius, Ray Daniels, and Tunji Balogun—thank you for your guidance, insights, and belief in my potential. Your support has been invaluable along the way.

To Adam Zia, my lawyer and trusted ally, for always having my back.

I'm inspired daily by the artists and creatives I've had the privilege to know and work with: Mallory Merk, Breez Kennedy, Damon "Dee" Gomes, Leven Kali, Genia, Annabelle Kline-Zilles, Dave Pensado, Sam Dhawan, and Ray Keys—your creativity and unique perspectives push me to be better each and every day.

To the executives who have uplifted me: Ashley Calhoun, a friend who provided the opportunity for my first-ever executive role, Maria Egan, Scott Cutler, Josh Abraham, Delmar Powell, Elias Leight, and Heran Mamo—thank you for seeing the value in my perspective and amplifying my voice.

A heartfelt shout-out to the students and upcoming professionals from Live Nation's Music Forward event: Quentin Hollis (organizer), Tiffany Fang, and Bella Mullin—your energy and passion are reminders of why I do this.

Lastly, to everyone who believed in me, challenged me, or shared their journey with me—you have all played a part in shaping mine. Thank you.